TESTAMENT OF SOME FORMER THINGS

John Scotus Eriugena

Translated by: D.P. Curtin

Dalcassian
Publishing
Company

PHILADELPHIA, PA

ISBN: **978-1-960069-70-2** (Paperback)

Library of Congress Control Number:
Author: Curtin, D.P. (1985-)

Front cover image: *Irish SeriesB Five Pound Note, Republic of Ireland*
Book design by J.J. Ripplestick

Printed by Ingram Content Group, 1 Ingram Blvd, La Vergne, Tennessee

First printing edition 2022.

Introduction

A cursory glance at this text would make it abundantly clear that it is attributed to John Sctous, and not written by him. It appears to be a collection of short recollections about his life, and perhaps more importantly, his death, as composed by some 17th century English author. This work does not appear along other works by Scotus found in the *Patrologia Latina* and is therefore likely a later composition from a non-Catholic library.

The context for its composition is not clear. However, the utilization of Latin here is specific to that which was promulgated at Cambridge following the Reformation. We might presume based upon the citations that are made that our true author was an English scholar who wants to render a polemic against those who claim that Scotus was Irish. This appears to be a poorly structured argument, and one that is flatly false, as 'Scotus' is unequivocal in meaning "Irish". Nevertheless, some Englishman sought to complete this glossary in an attempt to either prepare a book for such a discussion, or perhaps as lecture notes relating to their time in the university. The print source from this document dates from 1681 but is perhaps older than that. The resistance to Scotus being an Irishman might itself be an artifact from the War of Three Kingdoms, wherein the Irish were cast as mindless barbarians in the English imagination- a prejudice which has been survived in some English collegiate circles to down to the present day.

D.P. Curtin
February 21, 2022
Glen Mills, PA

TESTAMENT OF SOME FORMER THINGS
(Testimonia Aliquot Veterum)

Prudentius Tricassinus in his book against John the Scot:

"Ironically, Ireland has sent you only the sharpest of all Gauls."

Parduius, bishop of Laudun, about John Scotus:

"Since these things disagreed very much with each other, we forced that Scot who is in the king's palace [Charles the Bald] to write by the name of John."

From the history of the Antissiodorean bishops:

"Humbald of Cameracensis, highly instructed in the studies of the liberal arts, learned from John the Scot, who at that time shed rays of wisdom through Gaul, He became a footman, adhering to his discipline for a period, both divine and human."

Chronicon anonymous at Chesnius, Tomo III:

"At Aelfrid's request John Scotus returned from France, where he had been with Charles the Bald."

Roger of Wendover in the Chronicle to the year 883:

"In the year 883, the teacher John Scotus, a man of perspicacious genius, came to England."

Written, as it seems, from the life of Grimbald the abbot by Gotcelius:

"King Aelfrid, by the advice of Archbishop Eldred of Canterbury, sent orators to the Monastery of St. Bertini, about the arrival of Grimbald, among whom John the priest and Asserius were eminent men of the most learned and lively minds."

Annales Hydense:

"In the year of Our Lord's incarnation 886 AD, in the second year of St. Grimbald's arrival in England, the University of Oxford was begun—in Sacred Theology read by St. Neotus & Grimbald—in Grammar most true & Rhetoric, Asserius the Monk—in Dialectic & Verily Music & Arithmetic, John the Monk of Menevens Church, and in Geometry & Astronomy taught by John the Monk & his colleague St. Grimbaldi"

William Malmesbury in the fifth book on the Popes, unpublished:

"In the time of this Alfred, John Scotus came to England, a man of perceptive wit and much acumen, who, after leaving his native went to France, where he had passed over to Charles the Bald, by whom he was received with great dignity by his court. He appeared to him both serious and playful and was an individual companion of the king in both the dining table and court chamber. Many jokes and ingenuity of the hare were had, examples of which remain today, such as these: He had seated himself at the table opposite the King, on the part of the table; as the cups and dishes were consumed, Charles, with a cheerful face, after dinner, when he saw that John had done something which offended the Gallic courtesies, reprimanded him politely, and said, 'What separates a Sottus (a drunk) and a Scottus (an Irishman)?' He returned a solemn insult to the author and answered: 'Only the table'. The King had asked about a different subject, John had answered about the distance of the place, nor indeed was the King moved, because, taken by the miracle of his knowledge, he did not want to rise against the Master without being told, so he called him as he did. Likewise, when the attendant minister had presented to the King a dish containing two very large fishes, with one small one added, he gave them to the Master to divide with the two clerics who were reclining next to him. The fish were gigantic in size. John himself was close to them physically. Then he who always found something honourable to excite the joy of the guests, retaining for himself the two larger ones, distributed the smaller ones to the two clerics. He touched the two large fishes, and turned to the two great and large clerics, and one small one, and continued touching the fish. At the request of Charles, therefore, he translated the Hierarchy of Dionysius the Areopagite into Latin from the Greek, word for word. Now it happens that any Latin letter was scarcely understood, as it is understood better in Greek than our own tongue. He also composed a book which they call '*Peri Physion Merismus*', that is, '*On the Division of Nature*'. He did this because of the complexity of certain questions it is very useful to solve, if he may be forgiven in some places in which he deviated from the path of the Latins, while he fixed his eyes sharply on the Greeks. When he was accused of heresy, and a certain Florus wrote against him, for there are indeed in the book a very large number of views, which, unless they are carefully discussed, are seen to be repugnant to the faith of Catholics. Pope Nicholas is known to have shared this opinion, who says in his Epistle to Charles, 'It was reported to our apostleship that the work of the Blessed

Dionysius the Areopagite, which he described in Greek discourse on the divine names or heavenly orders, was recently translated into Latin by a certain man John of the Irish race. According to our custom, this was sent to us and in our judgment should have been approved, especially since this same John, although formerly said to be of great knowledge, is said to be not wise in some frequent rumors. Because of this infamy, I believe, he became weary of France, and he came to King Alfred, chosen by his generosity, and his scribal skills, as I understood the King's writings to be sublime. He settled in Meldun, where after some years, having been pierced with arrows by the boys whom he was teaching, he took his life with a heavy projectile. While the strong iniquity and the weak hands were often frustrated, and often attacked, he suffered a bitter death. He lay for some time in an honorable burial in the church of Blessed Lawrence, who had been acquainted with the strange woman. When the divine favor blessed him with a fiery light for many nights, the monks, being warned, transferred him into the greater church, and placing him to the left of the altar, preached his martyrdom in these verses.

> *Saint John the Sophist is buried in this tomb.*
> *He was already rich, living by a wonderful principle.*
> *At last the martyrdom of Christ ascended the kingdom,*
> *By which, he deserved, all the saints reign throughout the ages.*
> *The same William in the same book.*

Turald was replaced by Warinus de Lira, a monk. When he first came to the abbey of Malmsbury, rested on the laurels of his predecessors, a certain typhoid and nausea hung about the bodies of the saints where they were carried. Finally, the bones of the holy memory of Meildulphus and several others, who were formerly Abbots there, and later Antistites, were taken out of reverence for their patron Aldelmi, and were ordered to be buried in the place, which antiquity had reverently established to be venerated in two stone basins on either side of the altar, placed between each bone at intervals of wood. These things, I say, were all gathered together like a pile of garbage, like the remains of lowly slaves, alienated at the doors of the church. And in order that there might be no want of impudence, he also exalted St. John Scotus, whom the monks worshiped with almost the same veneration as St. Aldelmus. All these bodies were moved into the extreme corner of the basilica of St. Michael, where he imprudently commanded them to barricade them with stones. O times, O manners! Who is worthy of reproach to pursue such audacity?

From the same from Codex Thuaneus Manuscript- His Peter, his William, sharers in the divine philosophy:

You behave, most loving brother, in the manner of brotherly love, because you condescend to consult me so arduously. For it is a presumption of charity, that you think me not unfit for so great an office. For you order me to put into letters the place where John Scotus came from, where he died, the author of the book, which is called [...], according to common opinion. First, as I think, I will do well if I do this at once, because the truth of such things will not be hidden from me. Secondly, that a man most famous in the Latin world for the merit of his knowledge, and long life, and free from envy as the voice of justice, is deeper than my strength dares to breathe. For I also naturally shrink from being intrigued by the labors of the highest men, because, as some say, 'he who is clever in another's book acts unwisely'. Therefore, it was because of this, that I should have been opposed to such imperious commands, had it not long been settled in my mind that I should submit to you in all things, as a dear parent, even in those things which would burden my mind, and which might result in the danger of my shame. John, therefore, supposing that he was a native of his race, under the surname of Scotus, argues that he himself is mistaken, who calls himself 'Heruligena' in the title of the Hierarchy. Now the Heruli race was once the most powerful in Pannonia, and history shows that it was almost destroyed by the Lombards. Here he left his country, and came to France to Charles the Bald, with whom he was received with great dignity, and was regarded as part of his family, and spent time with him, as I have said elsewhere, in both serious and playful affairs, and was an individual companion both of the table and of the court chamber. Therefore, at the request of the king, he translated the Hierarchy of Dionysius from Greek into Latin, word for word, as Latin is scarcely understood. The text was written by a more Greek comprehension of things, than by that of our position. He composed a book which he entitled, that is, On the '*Division of Nature*', for the solution of certain perplexing questions, a very useful one, if he may be forgiven in some cases, in which he deviated from the path of the Latins, while he fixed his eyes too much on the Greeks. There was much reading and curiosity, sharp but inelegant, as I said, for the interpretation of knowledge. I think that he (to use the words of Anastasius, the librarian of the Roman Church) did not do so for any other reason than because, being humble in spirit, he did not presume to abandon the propriety of the word, lest in any way he should fall away from the sense of truth. They learned to envy him, like the mercenaries of the Greeks, who sprinkled in his books many things which the ears of the Latins would not receive. And not being ignorant of how envious these things were to his readers, he hid either under the person of dialogue, or under the mantle of Greek. For this reason, they thought he was a heretic, and a certain Florus wrote against him. For there are many things in the book which, in the estimation of many, seem to be removed from the Catholic faith. It is known that Pope Nicholas was of this opinion, who said in his Epistle to Charles, 'It was reported to our Apostolate that the work of the blessed Dionysius the Areopagite, which he described in Greek by the divine names or the heavenly orders, was recently translated into Latin by a certain John of the race of the Irish, which he sent to us according to custom, and ought to have been approved by our judgment.

Especially since the same John, although he is said to be very learned, was once said not to be wise in frequent rumors. Therefore, let your energy supply what has hitherto been omitted, and send us the aforesaid work without any hesitation.' Because of this infamy, as I believe, he became weary of France, and he came to England to King Alfred, whose generosity he elected, and his scholarly mastery, as I understood from his writings, resided in the high places of Malmesbury. When, after some years, he was pierced with a sword by the boys of whom he was teaching, he took his life with a heavy and bitter *coup de grace*. So while strong iniquity and weak hands were often frustrated, and often attacked, he would suffer a bitter death. He lay for some time in that church, which had been aware of his perverse death. Yet, when the divine favor blessed him with a fiery light for many nights, the monks, being warned, transferred him to the greater church, and to the left side of the altar, they preached of the martyr with these verses:

> St. John the Sophist was buried in this tomb.
> He who had been rich while living already with a wonderful principle.
> By martyrdom he finally deserved to ascend to heaven,
> In which the Saints always reign throughout the ages.

Anastasius praises Charles, who is still alive, for his remarkable sanctity. It is also to be wondered at how that barbarian man, by whom I mean John, who was born at the ends of the world, was in conversation with such men, and could be believed to be so distant from the speech of another language but was able to understand such things and translate them into another language. This work was done by that craftsman of spirits who made him both inspired and silver tongue, for unless he had been burning with the fire of charity out of grace, he would certainly not have received the gift of speaking in tongues. For this teacher was taught by charity, which he accomplished for the instruction and edification of many pupils. Therefore, they alternately write different things about his praises and infamies, although they always emphasize his greatness. The artist's eloquence was so great that all Gaul gave his hand to his great scholarly skill. It is true some desired greater boldness, such as the Synod which was assembled in the time of Pope Nicholas II at Tours. They cast a harsher sentence not on him, but on his writings. These, then, are generally the things which give rise to controversy.

John Pyke in his book on the Kings of the Anglo-Saxons:
Alfred learned of St. Grimbald and others with him through ambassadors. Many of those in Mercia, and in the uttermost parts of the earth, whom he knew how to rule, he attracted into his kingdom, and enlarged it with honors.

John Rous in the Book of Kings:
King Aluredus, St. Grimbald, a Flemish monk from the monastery of St. Bertini came, with associates John, Asserius & John of Wallense from the monastery of St. David accompanied him.

John of Tritenhem in the book of Ecclesiastical Writers:
John, called Erigena, a monk learned in the divine scriptures, and most learned in the discipline of secular literature, thoroughly instructed in Greek and Latin eloquence, subtle ingenuity, composed in speech, et cetera.

John Leland in book two of the British Writers:
Alfred, Plegmund, Werefrid, Asserius, Menevens, Grimbald, John, a monk from Saonia beyond the sea, and John Scotus, who interpreted the Hierarchy of Dionysius, had him in esteem and familiarity. These are the pieces of evidence which seemed to me to point most definitely to this John Scotus. What Baleus wrote about his father Patrick, about the pilgrimage he made to Athens, about

his wonderful skill in the eastern languages, will not gain any credence from me. Since that surname, 'Erigena', which is attributed to our John, is not yet sufficiently understood, as it seems to me. Let me, therefore, make my guesses about him.

Therefore, what William of Malmesbury says in the Epistle cited above, that Scotus called himself Heruligenes in the title of Hierarchy, I do not easily admit as true, as all the books with one mouth, as it were, they contradict him, and constantly bring before them either Erigena or Eriugena. William had read that John, a certain Ealdsaxon, had been with Alfred at Asserium and Ingulf. So much so, because the Heruli were once a nation in ancient Saxony, he thought this John to be descended from the Heruli. If, however, one believes that these did not fall out at random from Malmesbury, it must also be noted that the ancient writers report that the Heruli once settled among the Irish. In this matter, Latius can be consulted about the migrations of nations, and Beatus Rhenanus, whom he calls to the parties.

I am no more convinced of the opinion of those who, from this term Erigena, make John the Irishman. For more often in ancient books it is called Eriugena than Erigena; certainly, in the codex of the last antiquity (which is now preserved in the Library of the College of St. Trinity in Cantabria) which was used by Usserius Armachanus and I too, it is written Eriugena, not Erigena. So also, in Suffridus Peter, and so with Dionysius Petavius who we find in his own work, and so with Philip Labbeus. The word Erin, an Irishman, produces, not Erigena, but Erinigena, in which case P. Marca correctly painted that diction in the Epistle concerning this written by John to Luca Dacherius. Nor should anyone be moved by the fact that this John Hibernus is often called. This happened because the grace of studies had long been engaged in that nation, which at that time was the factory of good letters. Rossus, in his book on Kings, quotes from an ancient writer these things about Ireland. English studies had been suspended [by Gregory I, from the time of Augustine], and science flourished in Scotland and Ireland. Indeed, Ireland was at that time the fountainhead and pupil of all knowledge. St. Cedda studied there, first a disciple of St. Aidan, Bishop of Lindiffern, then Bishop of Ebor, and finally Bishop of Lindesia and all of Mercia. Egbertus was a fellow student in Ireland. I said that he was therefore said to have been Irish, because there he gave attention to letters. The same thing happened to a certain Marcus, who was commonly called an Irishman, although he was a Briton. Yet, he was brought up in Ireland, as Ericus of Antissiodorensis writes about him at the end of book one of the miracles of St. Germanus. The same thing happened to St. Patrick, Pelagius, and many others.

So that I may include my conjecture in a few. I think that this John, called Erigena, was from the place, apparently, named from his birth. Ergene is regarded as part of the county of Hereford, bordering on Wales. In the first place, one of the kingdoms of Wales was at this time, tributary to Alfred. In this tract I find the place of Eriuven, which indeed differs little from Eriugen (and by contraction Ergene). He who has observed how many changes are usually made in other barbarian dialects by twisting them to the Latin norm, will not hesitate to grant me these slight alterations in this voice. Indeed, the Book of the Church of Landau in Volume III of the Anglican Monastics, and Giraldus of Cambrian in his description of Cambria, chapter III, will teach more fully about this region. He notes that the diocese of Meneven was a part, where Asser was the archbishop, who was a relative of Asser, who heard John Erigenas teaching. The Book of Domesday also mentions this province, in which I read as follows: 'These were the customs of the T.R.E. of Wales in Archenefeld, i. e. Ergene.' Further, he notes that in both Giraldus and the Book of Landau, the Scots once occupied the borders of the Walls- whence the surname of our John the Scots may have come. Yet, I digress. These things also seem to be confirmed by the fact that John Erigena is called by the Scribes eloquently Wallus. So is noted by the composer of the Annals of Hydene, and so by Rossus in the book on kings. No, he himself does not obscurely allude to Wallus, in the poem to Charles the Bald—*Advena Joannes Spendo mio Carlo*. The voice of Wallus and the stranger are equivalent. He who wrote the life of Grimbald, reveals that John was sent as an ambassador to Flanders with Asser, to invite Grimbald, under the name of Alfred. It is not without probability that Master John died on this mission with his pupil. John had heard through Fulcon (now, in the year 882 AD. Archbishop of Remens, late Abbot Bertinianus) of the fame of Grimbald Bertinianus. When he returned to England in 883 AD, he had recommended the same to Alfred. Hence that mission followed in that year, or thereabouts, in 884 AD. Grimbald landed here in the year 885. These words are said so that no one should think that Erigena was stuck in Gaul at this time. More on this matter soon.

Finally, it may be asked by those who contend that this John was Irish by race and house, why he alone of so many of his people was surnamed Erigena. To this the Saxon Annals testify, Ericus of Antissiodorus testifies, and others among the most learned James Ussher, Archbishop of Armagh, in the Preface to the Irish Epistles, that many Irish (or Irish-Scots) had become acquainted with the literate world, at the time of Charlemagne, Charles the Bald, Alfred, & afterwards. None of whom, however, bear this name, Erigena, or are recognized as a gentile attribute. For they all hear either Irish or Scots, and Scots-Irish.

I come now to review the writings of Scotus Erigena. Now I place in the first place those works of man, concerning which no ambiguity is found among the ancients. That John therefore published:

1. On the Eucharist, book I

2. Versions of Dionysius Areop. book IV. viz. Of the Heavenly Hierarchy On the Ecclesiastical Hierarchy. Of the Divine Names. On Mystical Theology.

3. De Predestinatione adversus Goteschalcus, book. I

4. Versions of St. Maximus of the Ambiguus of St. Dionysius & Gregory the Theologian.

5. Treatises on the Vision of God

6. On the Division of Nature, book V

7. Letters

8. Versus

These are attributed to the same, which are under-noted.

9. Commentary on the Martian Chapel

10. Excerpts from Macrobius

11. On the Discipline of Scholars, Book I

12. Some discussion with Theodore Studita

13. Version of Aristotle's Morals

14. A version of Aristotle's book on the Regimine Principum

15. Commentaries on Aristotle's Sermons

16. Dogmas of the Philosophers

17. Homily

18. On Faith against the Barbarians

19. Paraphrastic Tomes, or Commentaries on Dionysius the Areopagite

1. Some think that the first of these Opusculos was interrupted. While others still wish to exist under the name of Bertram, or Ratramni. In addition to others, Peter of Marca can be consulted on this matter in *Luke Dacherius*

Spicilelius Tom. 2. And the learned man John Mabillonius in Praefat. to the second part of the 4th century *Acts of the Benedictines.*

2. Versions of Dionysius exist in Manuscripts, some of whom I saw were of the same century in which John lived. Scotus, as far as conjecture may reach. On these see Anastasius the Librarian, and Philip Labbeus in Anastasius *Bibliography.* There are also types of errors. Some observe that, on account of this version, John first came under suspicion of having little sound faith.

3. The third writing on predestination was printed in Paris in the year of our salvation, AD 1000. You have fifty among the writers of the 9th century, and among the writers of the Royal Council, Gilbert Mauguinus. with various judgments and criticisms of the ancients concerning that book.

4. St. Maximus wrote an exposition of some ambiguous passages which occur in the books of St. Dionysius and Gregory of Nazianzus. John Erigena translated these ambiguities into Latin. I do not know whether it is the whole work of Maximus, since I have not yet learned the complete Greek of St. Maximus. What I have received here at the end of the law, relate with me, partly with the favor of Emericus Bigotius, who examined what was written for my use from the Library of the King of the Gauls, and partly with my book, which contains many of the saying of the same Maximus. For the rest, to return to Scotus, his translation, which I am giving here, was shared with me by the kindness and learning of the famous John Mabillon. of which I have mentioned above. This version, apart from those which are easily observed in the books on the *Division of Nature*, sufficiently shows that Erigena was clearly alphabetic among the Greeks.

5. The same Mabillonius discovered a book *On The Vision of God* in a manuscript in the codex of Claromariscensi near Audomaropolin, with this title and beginning, *The Treatise of John Scotus on the Vision of God*. All the senses of the body are born from the conjunction of soul and body. I have endeavored that this book of Scotus should reach me, but my efforts have not yet been met with success.

6. I am now the first to read *Book V. on the Division of Nature*. These were supplied to me by my friend at the library. This book appears to have been written six hundred years ago. I did not think it safe enough to trust a single model, especially in writing subject to controversies. In the first place, I did not carelessly examine the passages which Scotus brought from the ancient fathers. When the book obtained some corrections, then, when I returned to Paris to the Monastery of St. Germain, I found that another copy of this work was preserved (and perhaps the only one according to that of my own. For the codex of Thuan was very mutilated.) By the grace of friends (among whom the first was Petrus Alixius) I obtained variant readings from this manuscript. Parisians, which, indeed, either the haste of our scribes, or the deficiency of the code itself, supplied the multiple errors. If anyone hereafter makes any edition from a copy of this manuscript, he will observe the discrepancies. Let them know that this happened, not on purpose, but by chance. Not by effort, not by fraud, but by human weakness, which does not see all things, that these errors have crept in. Abbot Trithemius ascribes these five books to John Scotus, whom they call Mailrosius. Baleus followed him, and wandered as he wandered. For, to say nothing of the Historians, (who indeed all unanimously ascribe this work to Scotus Erigena), it is quite clear from the version of the Ambiguus that the father of both works is one and the same. For a long time, no doubt, these books were circulated without the name of the author. All loved him. They also missed the Parisian pad. Nay, the name of the author was so unknown, that the work was condemned by the Parisians before it was

composed, of whom it was the fruit. Martinus Polonus thus writes of him (I read two manuscripts of the Reverend in Christ. William Archbishop Cantubury) This book is placed among other books condemned by the Parisians and is called the book of Amalric. These last words do not appear in the published books of Martin Poles. William of Malmesbury was the first to avenge this author, Erigena, as it is fair to suppose, admitted here to his own people that which he had been concealed from foreigners.

7. As far as I know, no one has seen any of Scotus's letters, except those which he prefixed to his books. Yet, it cannot be doubted that he wrote other things. I have placed at the foot of this volume an unpublished Epistle, which Erigena wrote to Charles the Bald, and a version to St. Maximus.

8. I would gladly have omitted the verses, had not Baleus thought them worthy to mention. Some are in the Calce Epistles to the book on Predestination, others are said to have been converted to the Areopagetic by Scotus. There are also some in the Glossary of Labbei, which Cangius brought to light. Finally, some poems by Scots to Charles are found in the Benedictine Codex manuscript, somewhere in Cambridge, which, may be the same as those which the Reverend Usser published long ago.

The following are also attributed to Scotus Erigena; correctly or incorrectly, I will not define:

9. Commentary on the Martian Chapel. Some commentaries on the chapel are preserved in a fairly ancient hand, in the extensive Library. By the men, Cotton, andBaronetti, yet they are anonymous, and for some reasons, I think they should rather be ascribed to Duncan the Irish Pope. Duncan is preserved in the library of our King Charles II.

10. Of the excerpts from Macrobius, the most famous Armachus James Usser, is also supposed to be extracts from those which are written among Macrobius, concerning the differences and associations of the Greek and Latin words.He said these things in the Irish Epistle.

11. On the discipline of scholars. He thinks that this John was written by Bouleus in the *History of the Academy of Paris*. Indeed, I think otherwise. For although our Scotus was a barbarian, and placed at the ends of the world, as Anastasius the Librarian speaks of him. Certainly not so much, and the author of that pamphlet, nor the men of his age, would have ever given him the name of Chrysostom, if they had thought him just a potter.

12. The discussion with Theodore does not seem to have been studied by him, since Theodore was a little older than he could have reached the times of our Scotus. Then it seems that the discussion was held about the worship of images, which indeed was discussed in the time of Alcvinus and John the Scotus Mailros. This discussion, therefore, seems to belong to him rather than to Erigena. It is preserved, as I hear, in the most famous Library of the King of the Gauls.

13. I do not know whether Aristotle translated the morals into Latin. I suspect that this work belongs to Scots.

14. The Aristotelian version, as is supposed, of the book *On the Government of the Prince*, is not the work of this Scotus, whatever Baleus wrote most confidently. I have several copies of this book, I have seen others, in all of which the translator is called John Patricius of Spain. Many know that this is the same as the above work, which I will not go into.

15. Commentaries on Aristotle are the Predicament of this John, if I understand Hugh and Peter of St. Victor correctly. I know, however, that in a certain Catalog of the Library of Oxford, the same name is preferred by Scotus. I say nothing about these books you have not seen.

16. Dogmas of the Philosophers; 17. Homily; 18. Defying the barbarians are clearly all works unknown to me. If Baleus had seen it, he would certainly have joined the initiations.

19. Of the Periphrastic tomes, or of the *Commentaries on Dionysius*, I have nothing but a faint suspicion; but I suspect that it is John the Scythopolitan, whom Anastasius the Librarian translated, or a paraphrase of a certain Abbot of Vercellis.

Moreover, from the writings of John Erigena, let him who wishes to know what the judgment of ancient men was, read the writers of the Goteschalcian History, Vossius, Usserius, Mauguinus, Cellotius, and also Peter de Marca.

Mabillonium and Alixium, by what kind of death John perished:

William of Malmesbury taught us thus, but at what time he ceased to be among the living, he does not specify with certainty. It is clear from Roger Wendover that the Scot returned to England in the year of salvation, 883, or, as others say, in the year 884. The great Baron wrote that it was in this very year 883 that he was executed by fate. He commends the truth of his opinion to our only historical witnesses, who do not say so. They speak of his death in that year by a kind of anticipation. After several years (from 883) he died when he was pierced by a sword, says William of Malmesbury. In the second year after the arrival of Grimbald (he came to England in 885), Scotus of Oxford reads, if the Annals of Hyden are to be believed. Who is the first or the only one to affirm this. Of the rest of his life I have found nothing.

He died an undignified death. He wished to make a good posterity immortal, and therefore he celebrated his birthday for a long time on the 5th of November. Arnoldus Wion mentions him honorably in the *Tree of Life*. and notes that in the Roman Martyrology, which was printed in the year 1580, his place and honor were established for him completely. However, the following editions of the Martyrology completely withdrew him. It seems to me that John was born to such a fate, that he was subject to the ever-changing judgments of men about him. Anastasius the Librarian preaches the man as holy in all things, while others distinguish him as a liar, a fool, a madman, and a heretic. They say that the children of Malmesbury killed him. The monks built a tomb. Other abbots of his equal status regard him almost with the honor of Aldelmo, Warinus regards him as almost garbage. These people put him in their fasting, others expel him outright. Thus his reputation and name have been relapsing like a fever for a long time now.

The sole place of burial is agreed upon by all. The catalog of St. Stephen, buried in England (which is now preserved in the Benedictine college at Cambridge) writes of him thus, in Saxon letters. St. Maildunus, St. Aldelmus, and John the Wise rest in Mailmesburia. A certain old connotation which was once read in the Mertonian Library of Oxford—St. Aldelmus and John the wise rest in a place called Malmesbiri. A statue was also placed in honor of this John in the sanctuary of the Abbey of Malmesbury, with this inscription; John Scotus, who translated Dionysius from Greek into Latin. So Leland in the Journey. I had these things about John Erigena, which I would now like to say.

LATIN TEXT

Prudentius Tricassinus in libro suo adversus Joannem Scotum.

Te solum omnium acutissimum Galliae transmisit Hibernia. ironice.

Pardulus Laudunensis Episcopus de Jo. Scoto.

Sed quia haec inter se valde dissentiebant, Scotum illum qui est in palatio regis [Caroli Calvi] Joannem nomine scribere coegimus.

Ex historia Episcoporum Antissiodorensium.

Humbaldus Cameracensis liberalium artium studiis apprime instructus, Joannis Scoti, qui ea tempestate per Gallias sapientiae fundebat radios, factus pedissequus, cujus disciplinatui longo tempore inhaerens, divina simul & humana—didicit.

Chronicon anonymum apud Chesnium, Tomo III.

Rogatu Aelfridi Joannes Scotus rediit a Francia, ubi erat cum Carolo Calvo.

Rogerus Wendover in Chronico ad annum 883.

Anno 883. venit in Angliam magister Joannes Scotus, vir perspicacis ingenii.

Ex vita Grimbaldi abbatis per Gotcelium, ut videtur, scripta.

Aelfridus rex consilio Eldredi archiepiscopi Cant. Oratores misit ad Monasterium S. Bertini, de accersendo Grimbaldo, inter quos presbyter Joannes & Asserius viri eruditissimi & vivacissimi ingenii praecellebant.

Annales Hidenses.

Anno dominicae incarnationis 886, anno secundo adventus S. Grimbaldi in Angliam, incoepta est Universitas Oxoniae—in S. Theologia legentibus S.

Neoto—& Grimbaldo—in Grammatica vero & Rhetorica Asserio Monacho—
in Dialectica vero & Musica & Arithmetica Joanne monacho Menevensis
Ecclesiae; in Geometria & Astronomia docente Joanne Monacho & collega S.
Grimbaldi.

Willielmus Malmesb. in lib. v. de Pontificibus, inedito.

Hujus Elfredi tempore venit in Angliam Joannes Scotus, vir perspicacis ingenii
& multae facundiae, qui dudum relicta patria Francia ad Carolum Calvum
transierat, a quo magna dignatione susceptus familiarium partium habebatur,
transigebatque cum eo tam seria quam joca, individuusque comes & mensae &
cubiculi erat, multae facetiae ingenuique leporis, quorum exempla, hodie quae
constant, ut sunt ista; Assederat ad mensam contra Regem adaliam tabulae
partem; procedentibus poculis consumtisque ferculis, Carolus fronte hilariori
post quaedam alia cum vidisset Joannem quiddam fecisse, quod Gallicanam
comitatem offenderet, urbane increpuit, & dixit, Quid distat inter Sottum &
Scottum? Retulit ille solenne convitium in auctorem, & respondit; Tabula
tantum: interrogaverat Rex de morum differenti studio, responderat Joannes
de loci distante spatio; nec vero Rex commotus est, quod miraculo scientiae
ipsius captus adversus Magistrum nec dicto insurgere vellet, sic eum usitate
vocabat. Item cum Regi convivanti minister patinam obtulisset, quae duos
pisces praegrandes, adjecto uno minusculo, contineret, dedit ille Magistro ut
accumbentibus duobus juxta se Clericis departiretur. Erant illi Giganteae molis;
ipse perex ilis corporis. Tum qui semper aliquid honesti inveniebat ut laetitiam
convivantium excitaret, retentis sibi duobus majoribus, unum minorem
duobus distribuit, Arguenti iniquitatem partitionis Regi, imo inquit, benefeci
& aeque, nam hic est unus parvus, de se dicens; & duos grandes pisces tangens.
Itemque ad eos conversus, hic sunt duo magni Clerici immensi, & unus
exiguus, piscem nihilominus tangens. Caroli ergo rogatu Hierarchiam Dionysii
Areopagitae in Latinum de Graeco, verbum e verbo, transtulit. Quo fit ut vix

intelligatur Latina litera, quae volubilitate magis Graeca quam positione construitur nostra. Composuit etiam librum quem peri physion Merismu, id est de naturae divisione titulant, propter perplexitatem quarundam quaestionum solvendam bene utilem, si tamen ignoscatur ei in quibusdam, quibus a Latinorum tramite deviavit, dum in Graecos acriter oculos intendit. Quare & Haereticus putatus est, scripsitque contra eum quidam Florus, sunt enim revera in libro peri physion perplurima, quae nisi diligenter discutiantur, a fide Catholicorum abhorrentia videantur. Hujus opinionis particeps fuisse cognoscitur Nicolaus Papa, qui ait in Epistola ad Carolum, Relatum est Apostolatui nostro, quod opus B. Dionysii Areopagitae, quod de divinis nominibus vel coelestibus ordinibus Graeco descripsit eloquio, quidam vir Joannes genere Scotus nuper in Latinum transtulerit, quod juxta morem nobis mitti & nostro judicio debuit approbari, praesertim cum idem Joannes, licet multae scientiae esse praedicetur, olim non sane sapere in quibusdam frequenti rumore dicatur. Propter hanc ergo infamiam credo taeduit eum Franciae, venitque ad Regem Aelfredum, cujus munificentia illectus, & magisterio ejus, ut ex scriptis Regis intellexi sublimis, Melduni resedit, ubi post aliquot annos, a pueris quos docebat graphiis perforatus, animam exuit tormento gravi & acerbo, ut dum iniquitas valida & manus infirma saepe frustraretur, & saepe impeteret, amaram mortem obiret. Jacuit aliqua ndiu in honorabili sepultura in Beati Laurentii Ecclesia quae fuerat infandae coedis conscia; sed ubi divinus favor multis noctibus super eum lucem indulsit igneam, admoniti Monachi, eum in majorem Ecclesiam transtulerunt, & ad sinistram altaris ponentes, his martyrium ejus versibus praedicaverunt.

Conditur hoc tumulo sanctus Sophista Joannes.
Qui ditatus erat jam vivens dogmate miro;
Martyrio tandem Christi conscendere regnum,
Quo, meruit, regnant cuncti per secula sancti.

Idem Willielmus in eodem libro.

Turaldo substitutus est Warinus de Lira monachus—is cum primum ad abbatiam [Malmsb.] venit, Antecessorum facta parvi pendens, typho quodam & nausea [erga] sanctorum corpora ferebatur; ossa denique sanctae memoriae Meildulphi & ceterorum, qui olim Abbates ibi, posteaque in pluribus locis Antistites ob reverentiam patroni sui Aldelmi se in loco tumulatum iri jussissent, quos antiquitas veneranda in duabus lapideis crateris ex utraque parte altaris, dispositis inter cujusque ossa ligneis intervallis reverenter statuerat; Haec, inquam, omnia pariter conglobata velut acervum ruderum, velut reliquias vilium mancipiorum ecclesiae foribus alienavit. Et ne quid impudentiae deesset, etiam S. Joannem Scotum, quem pene pari qua S. Aldelmum veneratione monachi colebant, extulit. Hos igitur omnes in extremo angulo basilicae S. Michaelis—inconsiderate occuli lapidibusque praecludi praecepit. O tempora, O mores! quis digno improperio tantam prosequatur audaciam?

Idem ex Cod. Thuaneo MS. Petro suo, Willelmus suus, divinae philosophiae participium.

Fraternae dilectioni morem, frater amantissime, geris, quod me tam ardua consultatione dignaris. Est enim praesumtio caritatis, quod me tanto muneri non imparem arbitraris. Praecipis enim ut mittam in literas unde Joannes Scottus oriundus, ubi defunctus fuerit, quem auctorem libri, qui ⟨ in non-Latin alphabet ⟩ vocatur, communis opinio consentit: simulque quia de libro illo sinister rumor aspersit, brevi scripto elucidem quae potissimum fidei videantur adversari catholicae. Et primum quidem ut puto probe faciam si promte expediam, quia me talium rerum veritas non lateat: alterum vero, ut hominem orbi latino merito scientiae notissimum, diuque vita, & invidia defunctum in jus vocem, altius est quam vires meae spirare audeant. Nam &

ego sponte refugio summorum virorum laboribus insidiari, quia ut quidam ait, Improbe facit qui in alieno libro ingeniosus est. Quapropter pene fuit ut jussis tam imperiosis essem contrarius, , nisi jamdudum constitisset animo, quod vobis in omnibus deferrem, ut parenti gratissimo, in his etiam quae onerarent frontem, quae essent pudoris mei periculo. Joannes igitur cognomento Scottus opinantes quod ejus gentis fuerit indigena, erroris ipse arguit, qui se Heruligenam in titulo Hierarchiae inscribit. Fuit autem gens Herulorum quondam potentissima in Pannonia, quam à Longobardis pene deletam eorundem prodit historia. Hic relicta patria, Franciam ad Carolum Calvum venit, à quo magna dignatione susceptus, familiarium partium habebatur, transigebatque cum eo (ut alias dixi) tam seria, quam joca, individuusque comes tam mensae, quam cubiculi erat: nec unquam inter eos fuit dissidium, quia miraculo scientiae ejus Rex captus, adversus magistrum quamvis ira praeproperum, nec dicto insurgere vellet. Regis ergo rogatu Hierarchiam Dionysii de graeco in latinum, de verbo verbum transtulit, quo fit ut vix intelligatur latina, quae volubilitate magis graeca quàm positione construitur nostra. Composuit & librum quem, id est, de Naturae divisione titulavit, propter quarundam perplexarum quaestionum solutionem bene utilem, si tamen ignoscatur ei in quibusdam, quibus à Latinorum tramite deviavit, dum in graecos nimium oculos intendit. Fuit multae lectionis & curiosae, acris sed inelegantis, ut dixi, ad interpretandum scientiae; quod eum (ut verbis Anastasii Romanae Ecclesiae bibliothecarii loquar) non egisse aliam ob causam existimo, nisi quia cum esset humilis spiritu non praesumsit verbi proprietatem deserere, ne aliquo modo à sensus veritate decideret. Doctus ad invidiam, ut graecorum pedissequus, qui multa quae non recipiant aures latinae, libris suis asperserit: quae non ignorans quam invidiosa lectoribus essent, vel sub persona collocutoris sui, vel sub pallio graecorum occulebat. Quapropter & haereticus putatus est, & scripsit contra eum quidam Florus. Sunt enim in libro perplurima, quae multorum aestimatione à fide catholica exorbitare videantur.

Hujus opinionis cognoscitur fuisse Nicolaus Papa, qui ait in Epistola ad Carolum, Relatum est Apostolatui nostro quod opus beati Dionysii Areopagitae, quod d• divinis nominibus, vel Coelestibus ordinibus graeco descripsit eloquio, quidam vester Johannes genere Scottus nuper in Latinum transtulerit, quod juxta morem nobis mitti, & nostro debuit judicio approbari, praesertim cum idem Joannes, licet multae scientiae esse praedicetur, olim non sane sapere in quibusdam frequenti rumore diceretur. Itaque quod hactenus omissum est, vestra industria suppleat, & nobis praefatum opus sine ulla cunctatione mittat. Propter hanc ergo infamiam, ut credo, taeduit eum Franciae, venitque Angliam ad regem Aelfredum, cujus munificentia illectus, & magisterio ejus, ut ex scriptis ejus intellexi, sublimis Malmesburiae resedit. Ubi post aliquot annos a pueris quos docebat graphiis perfossus, animam exuit tormento gravi & acerbo; ut dum iniquitas valida & manus infirma saepe frustraretur, & saepe impeteret, amaram mortem obiret. Jacuit aliquandiu in Ecclesia illa, quae fuerat infandae caedis conscia; sed ubi divinus favor multis noctibus super eum lucem indulsit igneam, admoniti Monachi in majorem eum transtulerunt Ecclesiam, & ad sinistram altaris positm, his praedicaverunt versibus martyrem,

Conditus hoc tumulo sanctus Sophista Joannes,
Qui ditatus erat vivens jam dogmate miro;
Martyrio tandem meruit conscendere caelum,
Quo semper cuncti regnant per secula Sancti.

Sed & Anastasius de insigni sanctitate adhuc viventem collaudat his verbis ad Carolum, Mirandum quoque est quomodo ille vir barbarus, Joannem dico, ille qui in finibus mundi positus, quanto ab hominibus conversatione, tanto credi potuit alterius linguae dictione longinquus, talia intellectu capere, in aliamque linguam transferre valuerit, Joannem dico Scottigenam, virum, quantum comperi, per omnia sanctum. Sed hoc operatus est ille artifex spiritus qui hunc ardentem pariter & loquentem fecit; nisi enim ex gratia ipsius igne caritatis flagrasset, nequaquam donum linguis loquendi proculdubio suscepisset. Nam hunc magistra caritas docuit quod ad multorum instructionem & aedificationem patravit. Alternant ergo de laudibus ejus, & infamia diversa scripta, quamvis jampridem laudes praeponderaverint. Tantum artifici valuit eloquentia, ut magisterio ejus manus dederit omnis Gallia. Verum si qui majorem audaciam anhelant, ut Synodus, quae tempore Nicolai Papae secundi Turonis congregata est; non in eum, sed in scripta ejus duriorem sententiam praecipitant. Sunt ergo haec fere quae controversiam pariunt.—

Joannes Pyke in libro de Regibus Anglo-saxonum.

S. Grimbaldum aliosque cum illo per legatos [Alfridus] adscivit; plures de Mercia, & ultimis terrae finibus quos scientia pollere novit, in regnum suum alliciens, honoribus ampliavit.

Joannes Rossus in libro de Regibus.

Rex Aluredus S. Grimbaldum Flandrensem monachum de monasterio S. Bertini, cum consociis Joanne & Asserio; & Joannem Wallensem a monasterio S. David sibi univit.

Joannes de Tritenhem in libro de Scriptoribus Ecclesiasticis.

Joonnes dictus Erigena, monachus in divinis scripturis doctus, & in disciplina secularium literarum eruditissimus, graeco & latino ad plenum instructus eloquio, ingenio subtilis, sermone compositus &c.

Joannes Lelandus in libro 2. de Scriptoribus Britannicis.

Aelfridus Plegmundum, Werefridum, Asserium, Menevensem, Grimbaldum, Joannem monachum e Saonia transmarina oriundum, Joannem Scotum, qui Dionysii Hierarchiam interpretatus est, in pretio habuit & familiaritate.

Atque haec sunt ea testimonia, quae mihi visa sunt certissime hunc Joannem Scotum designare. Quae vero Baleus de hujus patre Patricio, de peregrinatione, qua Athenas petiit, de mira in linguis Orientalibas peritia scripsit, nullam apud me fidem impetrant. Quoniam autem cognomen illud, Erigena, quod Joanni nostro tribuitur, nondum satis, ut mihi videtur, intelligitur; promam meas de eo conjecturas.

Quod igitur ait Gulielmus Malmesburiensis in Epistola superius allata, Scotum se appellasse Heruligenam in titulo Hierarchiae, non facile pro vero admiserim; omnes enim Codices MSS. uno quasi ore, ei contradicunt, & perpetuo prae se ferunt aut Erigenam aut Eriugenam. Legerat Gulielmus apud Asserium & Ingulfum fuisse cum Alfredo Joannem quendam Ealdsaxonem; atque adeo, quia Heruli gens erant olim in antiqua Saxonia, hunc Joannem ex Herulis oriundum existimavit.

Si quis tamen credit ista non temere Malmesburiensi excidisse; faciat sane pro eo, quod Herulos inter Hibernenses olim consedisse veteres Scriptores tradant. Qua de re consuli potest Lazius de migrationibus gentium, & Beatus Rhenanus, quem in partes vocat.

Non magis mihi probatur eorum sententia, qui ex hoc vocabulo Erigena Joannem faciunt Hibernum. Nam & saepius in antiquis libris Eriugena dicitur, quam Erigena; certe in codice ultimae antiquitatis, (qui nunc servatur in Bibliotheca collegii S. Trinitatis Cantabr.) quo usus est Usserius Armachanus & ego quoque, scribitur Eriugena, non Erigena. Ita quoque Suffridus Petri, ita in suis reperit Dionysius Petavius, ita Philip. Labbeus. Et vox Erin, Hibernus, producit, non Erigenam, sed Erinigenam, quo quidem pacto recte eam dictionem pinxit P. Marca in Epistola de hoc Joanne ad Lucam Dacherium exarata. Nec movere quenquam debeat, quod hic Joannes Hibernus toties dicatur; id evenit, quoniam studiorum gratia in ea gente diu versatus erat, quae tunc temporis bonarum literarum officina fuit. Rossus in libro de Regibus ex quodam antiquo scriptore ista de Hibernia profert; Anglicanis studiis suspensis [per Gregorium I. ab Augustini tempore] florebat scientia in Scotia & Hibernia; erat vero Hibernia totius tunc scientiae promtuarium & alumna. Ibi studebat S. Cedda prius S. Aidani Lindiffernensis Episcopi discipulus, postea Eborum, & demum Lindeseiae & totius Merciae Episcopus; cui conscholaris fuit in Hibernia Egbertus.—& multi praeclari moribus & scientia viri de Anglia. Dixi eum ideo Hibernum fuisse dictum, quod ibi literis operam dederit. Idem accidit Marco cuidam, qui Hibernus communiter dicebatur, cum tamen esset natione Britto; educatus vero in Hibernia, ut de eo scribit Ericus Antissiodorensis in fine libri 1. de miraculis S. Germani. Idem accidit S. Patricio, Pelagio, aliisque multis.

Ut igitur paucis meam conjecturam complectar; opinor Joannem istum, Erigenam dictum fuisse, a loco, ut videtur, natali. Est autem Ergene pars non contemnenda Herefordensis comitatus, Walliae contermina. lmo, unum e regnis Walliae fuit hoc tempore, Alfrido tributarium. In hoc tractu reperio locum Eriuven, quae quidem dictio parum discrepat ab Eriugen (& contracte Ergene) Jam tota terra ab ipsis Wallis modernis dicitur Erynug, vel Ereinuc. Qui observaverit, quantae in aliis dictionibus barbaris ad normam Latinam detorquendis mutationes plerumque fiant, non aegre has leviusculas alterationes mihi, hac in voce, concedet. Enimvero Liber Ecclesiae Landavensis in Tomo 3. Monastici Anglicani, Giraldus quoque Cambrensis in Cambriae descriptione c. 3, plenius de hac regiuncula docebunt: Quorum hic notat fuisse partem dioeceseos Menevensis; ubi Asser fuit Archiepiscopus, qui fuit propinquus Asseri, qui Joannem Erigenam audivit docentem. Hujus quoque provinciolae meminit liber Doomesday, in quo sic lego: Hae consuetudines erant Wallensium T. R. E. in Archenefeld, i. e. Ergene. Notat porro tum Giraldus, tum liber Landavensis, Scotos Wallorum fines aliquando occupasse; unde & Joanni nostro Scoti cognomen potuit accessisse. Sed ut redeam. Haec etiam inde videntur confirmari, quod Joannes Erigena, à Scriptoribus diserte Wallus appelletur. Sic Hidensium Annalium compositor, sic Rossus in libro de regibus. Imo ipse se Wallum non obscure innuit, in carmine ad Carolum Calvum—Advena Joannes Spendo meo Carolo. Vox enim Wallus & advena aequipollent. Qui vitam Grimbaldi scripsit, prodit Joannem cum Assero legatum in Flandriam missum fuisse ad invitandum, Alfredi nomine, Grimbaldum. Non caret probabilitate magistrum Joannem cum suo discipulo hanc legationem obiisse. Audierat Joannes per Fulconem (nunc, anno 882. Archiepiscopum Remensem, nuper Abbatem Bertinianum) de fama Grimbaldi Bertiniani; redux ille in Angliam, anno 883, Aelfredo eundem commendaverat. Hinc sequuta est illa legatio, anno, vel circiter, 884; nam appulit huc Grimbaldus anno 885. Ista dicta sunt ne quis existimet Erigenam, hoc in tempore, in Galliis haesisse. Sed hac de re plura mox.

Denique, quaeri ab iis potest, qui Joannem hunc Hibernum gente & domo fuisse contendunt, cur hic solus e tot popularibus suis Erigena cognominatus fuerit. Testantur certe Annales Saxonici, testatur Ericus Antissiodorensis, aliique apud doctissimum Jac. Usserium Armac. Arch. in Praefatione ad Epistolas Hibernicas, perplures Hibernos (seu Scoto-Hibernos) orbi literato innotuisse, per Caroli magni, Caroli Calvi, Aelfredi tempora, & deinceps;

quorum tamen nemini nomen hoc, Erigena, pro gentili attributum cognoscitur. Omnes enim vel Hiberni, vel Scoti, & Scoto-hiberni audiunt.

Venio nunc ad Scoti Erigenae scripta recensenda. Pono autem primo loco ea hominis opuscula, de quibus nulla apud veteres reperitur ambiguitas. Edidit igitur Joannes ille

1. De Eucharistia librum I.

2. Versiones Dionysii Areop. lib. IV. viz. De Coelesti Hierarchia. De Ecclesiastica Hierarchia. De Divinis Nominibus. De Mystica Theologia.

3. De Praedestinatione adversus Goteschalcum, lib. I.

4. Versiones S. Maximi de Ambiguis S. Dionysii & Gregorii Theologi.

5. De Visione Dei Tractatum.

6. De Divisione Naturae, lib. V.

7. Epistolas.

8. Versus.

Tribuuntur eidem & haec, quae subnotantur.

9. In Martianum Capellam Commentarii.

10. Excerpta ex Macrobio.

11. De Disciplina Scholarium, liber I.

12. Disputatio quaedam cum Theodoro Studita.

13. Versio Moralium Aristotelis.

14. Versio libri Aristotelis de Regimine Principum.

15. Commentarii in Aristotelis Praedicamenta.

16. Dogmata Philosophorum.

17. Homiliae.

18. De Fide contra Barbaros.

19. Paraphrastici Tomi, sive Commentarii in Dionysium Areopagitam.

1. Horum Opusculorum primum putant aliqui intercidisse; alii adhuc extare volunt sub nomine Bertrami, vel Ratramni. Praeter alios hac de re consuli possunt Petrus de Marca apud Lucam Dacherium Spicilegii Tom. 2. &

doctissimus vir Ioan. Mabillonius in Praefat. ad 2. partem seculi 4. Act. Benedictinorum.

2. Versiones Dionysii extant, in Manuscriptis codd. quorum aliquot vidi, ipsius seculi, in quo vixit Joan. Scotus, quantum conjectura assequi liceat. De his vide Anastasium Bibliothecarium, & Philippum Labbeum in Anastasio Bibl. Extant etiam typis cusae. Observant nonnulli ob hanc versionem primo in suspicionem venisse Joannem fidei parum sanae.

3. Tertium scriptum de Praedestinatione Typis vulgatum Parisiis anno salutis nostrae M. DC. L. habes apud Regium Consiliarium Gilbertum Mauguinum inter scriptores seculi IX. cum variis de eo libro antiquorum judiciis & censuris.

4. S. Maximus scripsit expositionem Ambiguorum aliquot locorum, quae in S. Dionysii & Gregorii Nazianzeni libris occurrunt. Haec Ambigua Ioannes Erigena vertit latine. Nescio an totum Maximi opus: quoniam Graeca S. Maximi integra nondum nactus sum. Quae hic in fine legis, accepta mecum refer partim beneficio V. C. Emerici Bigotii, qui ex Bibliotheca Regis Galliarum in meos usus descripta examinavit, partim codici meo, qui complurimas ejusdem Maximi lucubrationes continet. Caeterum, ut redeam ad Scotum, ejus tralationem quam hic edo, mecum communicavit humanitate & eruditione celebris V. Ioannes Mabillon. de quo supra commemoravi. Haec versio, absque iis, quae in libris de Divisione naturae facile observantur, satis ostendit Erigenam fuisse in Graecis plane alphabetarium.

5. Idem V. C. I. Mabillonius librum de Visione Dei deprehendit in MS. codice Claromariscensi prope Audomaropolin, cum hoc titulo & initio, TRACTATUS Joannis Scoti DE VISIONE DEI. Omnes sensus corporei ex

conjunctione nascuntur animae & corporis. Dedi ego operam, ut ad me perveniret hic Scoti liber; sed conatui adhuc non respondit successus.

6. Libros V. de Divisione Naturae primus nunc edo. Hos mihi suppeditavit supellex mea, (curta alias) libraria. Codex noster videtur scriptus fuisse ante annos sexcentos. Quoniam autem non satis tutum existimavi unico fidere exemplari, praesertim in scriptione controversiis obnoxia; primo locos, quos Scotus ex antiquis patribus adduxit non indiligenter inspexi; unde nonnullas emendationes codex ille noster lucratus est: deinde, cum rescirem Parisiis in Monasterio S. Germani, hujus operis servari exemplar aliud (& forte unicum secundum illud meum; nam Codex Thuani valde mutilus erat) amicorum gratia (inter quos primus D. V. Petrus Alixius) obtinui variantes lectiones ex isto MS. Parisiensi: quae quidem seu scribae nostri festinationes seu codicis ipsius defectus multifariam suppleverunt. Si quis posthac aliquas in hac editione ab exemplari MS. discrepantias observaverit; sciat eas evenisse, non consulto, sed casu; non studio, non fraude mala, sed per humanam infirmitatem, quae non videt omnia, irrepsisse. Hos V. libros Abbas Trithemius adscribit Ioanni Scoto, quem Mailrosium vocant. Eum sequitur Baleus, & cum errante errat. Nam, ut de Historicis nihil dicam, (qui quidem omnes unanimiter hoc opus Scoto Erigenae ascribunt) satis constat ex versione Ambiguorum unum & eundem utriusque operis esse patrem. Diu haud dubie, sine auctoris nomine circumlati sunt hi libri; eo caruit noster; eo etiam Parisiensis codex caruit. Imo adeo ignorabatur nomen auctoris, ut opus prius damnatum fuerit Parisiis, quam constiterit, cujus esset foetus. Martinus Polonus sic de eo scribit (quemadmodum in duobus MSS. penes Reverendissimum in Chr. P. Gulielmum Archi-epis. Cantuar. legi) Hic liber inter alios libros condemnatos Parisiis ponitur, & dicitur liber Amalrici. Postrema haec verba non comparent in editis libris Mart. Poloni. Gulielmus

Malmesburiensis primus suo auctori vindicavit; Erigena, ut par est existimare, hic apud suos id fassus erat, quod apud exteros celaverat.

7. Epistolas Scoti nullas, quod scio, quisquam vidit, praeter eas quae libris suis praefixit; nec tamen dubitari potest, quin alias scripserit. Subjeci in calce hujus voluminis ineditam Epistolam, quam scripsit Erigena ad Carolum Calvum de S. Maximi versione.

8. Versus omisissem libenter, nisi hos dignos existimasset Baleus, quos commemoraret. Extant quidam in Calce Epistolae ad librum de Praedestinatione alii habentur praemissi ad Areopagetica à Scoto conversa. Sunt quoque nonnulli in Glossario Labbei, quod Cangius in lucem dedit. Reperiuntur denique aliquot Scoti ad Carolum carmina in Codice MS. Benedictino apud Cantabrigienses; quae tamen eadem forte sunt cum iis, quos Reverendissimus Usserius jamdudum publicavit.

Tribuuntur Scoto Erigenae etiam haec, quae sequuntur opuscula; recte an secus, non definio.

9. In Martianum Capellam Commentarii. Servantur commentarii quidam in Capellam satis antiquae manus, in Bibliotheca ampliss. viri J. Cotton, Baronetti: sed anonymi sunt, & ob nonnullas rationes, puto Dunchanto Pontifici Hibernensi potius esse adscribendos. Dunchantum servat Bibliotheca Regis nostri Caroli II.

10. De excerptis ex Macrobio sic clarissimus Armach. Jacobus Usserius; Joannis quoque nostri putantur esse excerpta illa quae inter Macrobii scripta feruntur,

de differentiis & societatibus Graeci Latinique verbi &c. Ita quoque censuit P. Pithaeus V. Cl. Haec ille in Epist. Hibernicis.

11. De disciplina Scholarium. Putat Joannem hunc scripsisse Buleus in Historia Academiae Parisiensis. Equidem aliter censeo. Quanquam enim Scotus noster barbarus erat & in finibus mundi positus, ut de eo loquitur Anastasius Bibliothecarius; certe non adeo, ac auctor istius libelli, nec Chrysostomi nomen ei unquam tribuissent sui seculi homines, si istius scripti figulum existimassent.

12. Disputatio cum Theodoro Studita hujus esse non videtur, quoninam Theodorus paulo senior fuit, quam ut ad Scoti nostri tempora pertingere posset: deinde videtur illa disputatio celebrata fuisse de cultu imaginum, quae quidem agitabatur tempore Alcwini & Joannis Scoti Mailros. Huic igitur, potius quam Erigenae competere videtur ista disputatio: servatur, uti audio, in celeberrima Bibliotheca Regis Galliarum.

13. Moralia Aristotelis an Latine verterit nescio; suspicor alîus Scoti esse laborem illum.

14. Versio Aristotelici, ut putatur, libri de regimine Principum hujus Scoti non est opus, quicquid confidentissimus scripserit Baleus. Habeo aliquot istius libri exemplaria, vidi alia, in quibus omnibus, is qui vertit, dicitur Joannes Patricius Hispanensis. Multi hoc cum superiori opusculo idem esse sciscunt, quibus non accedo.

15. Commentarii in Aristotelis Praedicamenta sunt hujus Joannis 〈 in non-Latin alphabet 〉 , si Hugonem & Petrum de S. Victore recte capio. Scio tamen

in Catalogo quodam Bibliothecae Oxoniensis, eadem alîus Scoti nomen praeferre. Nihil de his pronuncio, libris non visis.

16. Dogmata Philosophorum; 17. Homiliae; 18. deFide contra Barbaros mihi plane sunt opera incognita omnia. Si vidisset Baleus, utique & initiahorum apposuisset.

19. De Paraphrasticis tomis, sive commentariis in Dionysium praeter tenuem suspicionem nihil habeo; suspicor autem esse Joannis Scythopolitani, quas vertit Anastasius Bibliothecarius; vel paraphrasin Abbatis cujusdam Vercellensis.

Porro de scriptis Joannis Erigenae quale fuerit antiquorum hominum judicium, qui scire avet, legat scriptores Historiae Goteschalcianae, Vossium, Usserium, Mauguinum, Cellotium, item Petrum de Marca, Joan. Mabillonium, & P. Alixium. Quo mortis genere periit Joan. docuit nos Gulielmus Malmesburiensis; quo autem tempore inter vivos esse desiit, non certo designat. Constat ex Rogero Wendovero Scotum in Angliam rediisse anno salutis 883. vel, ut alii, anno 884. Hoc ipso anno 883. fato functum esse scripsit magnus Baronius. Verum sententiae suae nostrates solos historicos testes laudat, qui id non dicunt; nam de ejus morte loquuntur eo anno per quandam anticipationem. Post aliquot annos (ab 883.) graphiis perfossus animam exuit, inquit Gulielmus Malmesburiensis. Secundo anno post adventum Grimbaldi (venit ille in Angliam anno 885.) legit Oxonii Scotus, si fides sit Annalibus Hidensibus; qui aut primi aut soli hoc affirmant. De reliquo vitae spatio nihil comperti habeo.

Periit indigna morte: grata posteritas immortalem efficere cupiit, ideoque ejus natale ad 4. Idus Novembris diu celebravit. Arnoldus Wion de eo in Ligno vitae, honorifice meminit; notatque in Martyrologio Romano, quod excudebatur anno 1580, ei locum & decus suum integrum constitisse, à quo tamen sequentes editiones Martyrologii eum penitus detraxerunt. Eo fato mihi natus fuisse Joannes videtur, ut hominum de se judicia semper alternantia subiret. Anastasius Bibliothecarius virum per omnia sanctum praedicat, alii ut mendacem, ineptum, dementem, haereticum differunt. Pueri Malmesburienses eum interficiunt; Monachi sepulcrum condunt. Abbates alii pari eum fere cum suo Aldelmo honore prosequuntur, Warinus pene pro purgamento habet. Hi eum fastis inserunt, alii expungunt. Ita ejus fama & nomen recidiva quasi febri jam diu conflictatur.

De solo sepulturae loco inter omnes convenit. Catalogus S. S. in Anglia sepultorum (qui nunc in collegio Benedictino apud Cantabrigienses servatur) de eo sic scribit, literis Saxonicis. S. Maildunus, S. Aldelmus, & Joannes sapiens requiescunt in Mailmesburia, Eadem habet Codex Cottonianus ex Gotcelino Bertiniano, nec abit ab his, uti vidimus, Malmesburiensis Bibliothecarius; nec vetusta quaedam connotatio quae olim legebatur in Mertoniana Bibliotheca Oxoniensi—S. Aldelmus & Joannes sapiens pausant in loco, qui dicitur in Malmesbiri. Fuit quoque in honorem hujus Joannes Statua posita in templo Abbatiae Malmesburiensis, cum hac inscriptione; Joannes Scotus, qui transtulit Dionysium e Graeco in Latinum. Ita Lelandus in Itinerario. Haec habui de Joanne Erigena, quae nunc dicerem.

The Scriptorium Project is the work of a small group of lay people of various apostolic churches who are interested in the preservation, transmission, and translation of the works of the early and medieval church. Our efforts are to make the works of the church fathers accessible to anyone who might have an interest in Christian antiquities and the theological, philosophical, and moral writings that have become the bedrock of Western Civilization.

To-date, our releases have pulled from the Greek, Syriac, Georgian, Latin, Celtic, Ethiopian, and Coptic traditions of Christianity, and have been pulled from sundry local traditions and languages.

Other Titles and Translations by D.P. Curtin:

First Book of Ethiopian Maccabees (2018)
Protoevangelium of James: Greek and English Texts (2019)
Edicts of the Synod of Paris by Chlothar II, King of Franks (2019)
The Life of St. Desiderius by Sisebut, King of Visigoths (2019)
The Synod of Rome by St. Boniface IV of Rome (2019)
Letter to Pope Theodore by Victor of Carthage (2020)
The Decree of 610 by Gundemar, King of Visigoths (2020)
Laws of the Church by Dagobert I, King of Franks (2020)
The Old Nubian Miracle of St. Mena (2021)
About Fifteen Problems by St. Albertus Magnus (2022)
Testament of Some Former Things by John Scotus Eriugena (2022)
The Georgian Synaxarium (2022)
Instructions: Counsel for Novices by St. Ammonas the Hermit (2022)
The Syriac Menologium and Martyrology (2022)
Book on Religious Exercise and Quiet by St. Isaiah the Solitary (2022)
Vision of Theophilus by St. Cyril of Alexandria (2022)
On Fate (De Fato) by St. Albertus Magnus (2023)
Fragments of 'Chronicle' by Hippolytus of Thebes (2023)
Life of the Blessed Theotokos by Epiphanius Monachus (2023)
Syriac Life of John the Baptist by Serapion the Presbyter (2023)
Second Book of Ethiopian Maccabees (2023)